Note to parents, carers and teachers

Read it yourself is a series of modern stories, favourite characters, traditional tales and first reference books written in a simple way for children who are learning to read. The books can be read independently or as part of a guided reading session.

Each book is carefully structured to include many high-frequency words vital for first reading. The sentences on each page are supported closely by pictures to help with understanding, and to offer lively details to talk about.

The books are graded into four levels that progressively introduce wider vocabulary and longer text as a reader's ability and confidence grows.

Ideas for use

- Ask how your child would like to approach reading at this stage. Would he prefer to hear you read the book first, or would he like to read the words to you and see how he gets on?

- Help him to sound out any words he does not know.

- Developing readers can be concentrating so hard on the words that they sometimes don't fully grasp the meaning of what they're reading. Answering the quiz questions at the end of the book will help with understanding.

For more information and advice on Read it yourself and book banding, visit www.ladybird.com/readityourself

Book Band 7

Level 3 is ideal for children who are developing reading confidence and stamina, and who are eager to read longer books with a wider vocabulary.

Special features:

Wider vocabulary, reinforced through repetition

Detailed pictures for added interest and discussion

Time to hibernate

When it gets cold, reptiles and amphibians look for a place to hibernate. This is when they have a very big sleep. They come out when it is not so cold.

Some reptiles, like these snakes, hibernate with others in a cool, dry place.

18

Amphibians, like these salamanders, hibernate in cool, wet places.

19

Flying frogs

Some frogs live up here in the trees.

When they jump it looks like they are flying from tree to tree.

Longer sentences

Captions and labels clarify information

The skin here helps them when they jump to get bugs on other trees.

32   33

Educational Consultant: Geraldine Taylor
Book Banding Consultant: Kate Ruttle
Subject Consultant: Steve Parker

LADYBIRD BOOKS

UK | USA | Canada | Ireland | Australia
India | New Zealand | South Africa

Ladybird Books is part of the Penguin Random House group of companies
whose addresses can be found at global.penguinrandomhouse.com.

www.penguin.co.uk www.puffin.co.uk www.ladybird.co.uk

First published 2017
This edition 2019
002

Copyright © Ladybird Books Ltd, 2017

Printed in China

A CIP catalogue record for this book is available from the British Library

ISBN: 978-0-241-40540-6

All correspondence to:
Ladybird Books
Penguin Random House Children's
One Embassy Gardens, 8 Viaduct Gardens, London SW11 7BW

Reptiles and Amphibians

Written by Zoë Clarke
Illustrated by Cherie Zamazing

Contents

Reptiles and amphibians

Reptiles and amphibians are animals. Some are big and some are not!

Reptiles

turtle

snake

lizard

crocodile

alligator

Amphibians

newt

frog —

salamander

toad

Cold-blooded

Reptiles and amphibians are
cold-blooded. Their bodies get
hot in the sun.

Their bodies cool down here,
out of the sun.

Wet skin

Amphibians have smooth, wet skin.

They make mucus
in their skin.

The mucus makes their skin wet.

Water makes their skin wet, too.

Scales and plates

Reptiles have dry skin. Water doesn't get in here! Some have lots of smooth scales all over them.

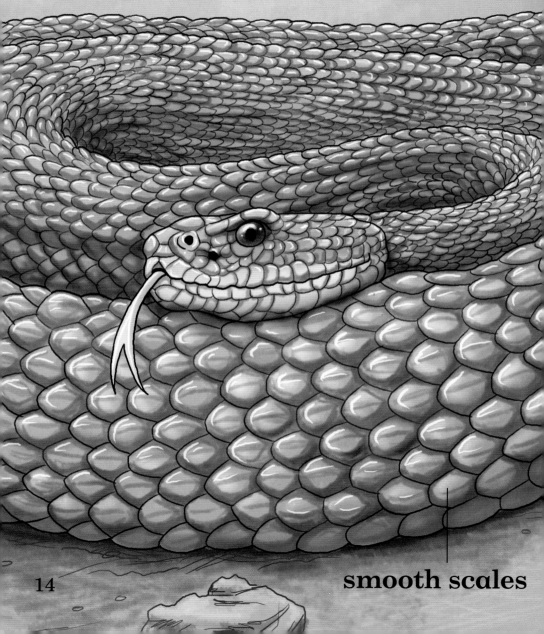

smooth scales

Some reptiles, like these,
have hard scales called plates.

hard plates

Home

Many reptiles live in hot, dry places, like deserts.

Some come out in the night, when it is cool.

Many amphibians live in wet places.
They live in water and on land.

Time to hibernate

When it gets cold, reptiles and amphibians look for a place to hibernate. This is when they have a very big sleep. They come out when it is not so cold.

Some reptiles, like these snakes, hibernate with others in a cool, dry place.

Amphibians, like these salamanders,
hibernate in cool, wet places.

Teeth to eat with!

Many reptiles eat other animals.
Big reptiles like crocodiles and
alligators have sharp teeth to bite with.

crocodile

There are over
60 teeth in here!

You can see lots of teeth in a
crocodile's mouth when it is closed.

alligator

There are over 70 teeth in here!

An alligator shows less teeth than a crocodile when its mouth is closed.

21

Get the bugs!

This lizard has a long tongue.
Little animals stick to it.

Amphibians eat animals, too.
They have little teeth, so they
eat bugs in one go!

Camouflage

There is a frog here. Here it is!
It looks like the place where it is
hiding – this is called camouflage.

Amphibians are safe hiding like this.

Some reptiles are good at hiding, too,
like this lizard.

Colour warning

These reptiles and amphibians don't go into hiding. Their skin colour is a warning to other animals.

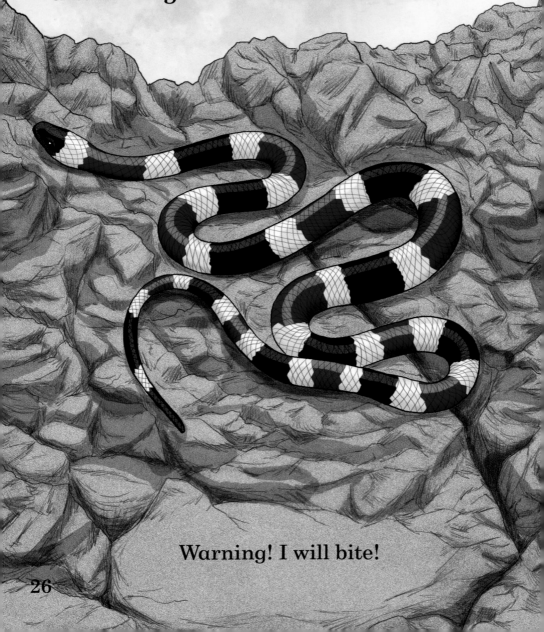

Warning! I will bite!

Warning! Not good to eat!

Spines, claws and teeth

There are spines on this lizard.
The spines are sharp, so other
animals don't want to eat it.

This big lizard has sharp claws!

This snake has 60 sharp teeth.

Slow, or go, go, go!

Some reptiles are slow like this one.

Some are not slow. They go!

lizard

Snakes' scales help them push and pull well to make them go.

push and pull

Flying frogs

Some frogs live up here in the trees.

When they jump it looks like they are flying from tree to tree.

The skin here helps them when they jump to get bugs on other trees.

See it, hear it, smell it

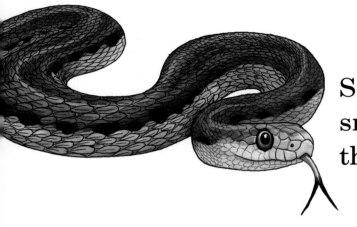

Snakes
smell with
their tongues!

Lizards
see well.

newt

Frogs,
salamanders
and newts hear
and smell well.

Turtles see and smell well.

crocodile

Crocodiles and alligators
see, smell and hear well.

Little reptiles

Reptiles lay eggs on land like this. Some crocodiles lay up to 80 eggs.

crocodile eggs

This turtle lays over 100 eggs!

Little amphibians

Many amphibians lay their eggs in water. As amphibians get big, they don't look the same.

Toad eggs look like this.

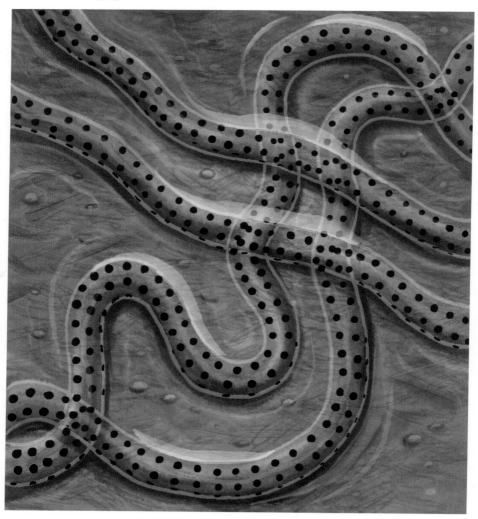

Then, toads look like this.

Then, like this!

What lives here?

This frog doesn't live like other amphibians. It lives in the desert.

The frog hides down here.

This snake doesn't live like other reptiles.
It lives in the sea.

sea snake

Help the reptiles and amphibians

Many reptiles and amphibians have no home.

It is up to us to help them and make them a good home.

This will be a good home!

Picture glossary

 alligator

 camouflage

 crocodile

 frog

 lizard

 newt

 plates

 salamander

 scales

 snake

 spines

 turtle

Index

Reptiles and Amphibians quiz

What have you learnt about reptiles and amphibians? Answer these questions and find out!

- Do reptiles and amphibians have cold or warm blood?

- Where do amphibians make mucus?

- What do some reptiles and amphibians use to hide away?

- What do snakes use to smell?

- What do reptiles and amphibians do when they hibernate?

www.ladybird.com